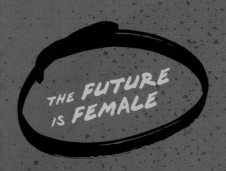

THE *FUTURE* IS *FEMALE*

Changemakers in
STEM

Women Leading the Way

DR. ARTIKA R. TYNER

Lerner Publications ◆ Minneapolis

This book is dedicated to Dr. Reatha Clark King, a pioneering scientist, educator, and servant leader.

Lerner Publications Company
An imprint of Lerner Publishing Group, Inc.
241 First Avenue North
Minneapolis, MN 55401 USA

For reading levels and more information, look up this title at www.lernerbooks.com.

Main body text set in Aptifer Sans LT Pro Medium.
Typeface provided by Linotype AG.

Editor: Brianna Kaiser **Designer:** Athena Currier
Lerner team: Martha Kranes

Library of Congress Cataloging-in-Publication Data

Names: Tyner, Artika R., author.
Title: Changemakers in STEM : women leading the way / Dr. Artika R. Tyner.
Description: Minneapolis : Lerner Publications, [2024] | Series: The future is female (alternator books) | Includes bibliographical references and index. | Audience: Ages 8–12 | Audience: Grades 4–6 | Summary: "Discover the women who have shaped the fields of science, technology, engineering, and mathematics. Readers will uncover women of the past and present who have made scientific breakthroughs, developed innovative technology, and more!"— Provided by publisher.
Identifiers: LCCN 2023010631 (print) | LCCN 2023010632 (ebook) | ISBN 9798765608906 (library binding) | ISBN 9798765625040 (paperback) | ISBN 9798765618462 (epub)
Subjects: LCSH: Women scientists—Juvenile literature. | BISAC: JUVENILE NONFICTION / Biography & Autobiography / Women
Classification: LCC Q130 .T96 2024 (print) | LCC Q130 (ebook) | DDC 509.2/52 [B]—dc23/eng20230722

LC record available at https://lccn.loc.gov/2023010631
LC ebook record available at https://lccn.loc.gov/2023010632

Manufactured in the United States of America
1-1009552-51568-7/7/2023

Table of Contents

Reaching Young Scientists

Computer scientist Pooja Chandrashekar was on a mission. In her first year of high school, she noticed a gender gap. She was only one of three girls in her computer science class. She wanted to change this.

In 2013, Chandrashekar's second year of high school, she founded ProjectCSGirls, a group that works to get middle school girls in STEM (science, technology, engineering, and mathematics). Each year, ProjectCSGirls holds a technology

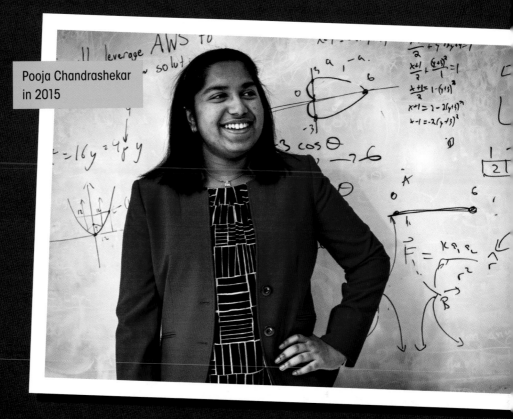

Pooja Chandrashekar in 2015

and computer science competition for girls. The group serves over fifteen thousand girls in over twelve countries.

Chandrashekar has given many talks about the need for women to work in STEM. Women in STEM create ideas and make positive changes in their communities. This book doesn't cover all women leaders in STEM. But the ones highlighted here are among those who inspire the next generation of women to make change.

CHAPTER 1

Discovering Ideas in Science

Scientists are always learning. They use their skills to find answers and improve our knowledge in different areas.

Mapping the ocean

Marie Tharp became a scientist when few women were scientists. Tharp studied Earth and wanted to learn more about the ocean floor. At the time, many people thought the bottom of the ocean was flat and did not shift over time.

In 1968 Marie Tharp (*right*) joins an expedition on the *USNS Kane* to collect data on the ocean floor.

In 1948 Tharp partnered with scientist Bruce Heezen to map the ocean floor. They completed an Atlantic Ocean map in 1957. Two decades later, they completed a map of the ocean floor for the world. Tharp's work supported the idea that the continents move over time.

One of Alondra Fraustro's inventions helps address droughts in South Korea.

planting for change

Award-winning scientist Alondra Fraustro found a love for science as a young girl. She won many competitions by the time she was fourteen years old.

She invented a gardening kit to help address droughts—a dry time with low amounts of water—in South Korea. For her invention, she won the 2020 United Nations' Champions of the

Earth award. Fraustro is also the founder of Ecobiores. The company works to reduce the use of plastics. Fraustro uses science to fight climate change and teach others about it.

Big Discoveries

In 1947 Marie M. Daly became the first Black woman to earn a PhD in chemistry in the US. A PhD is the highest level of college degree. She researched how proteins are made in the body and what causes heart attacks. She helped discover that

Marie Daly in 1942

high cholesterol, a waxy substance in blood, is connected to heart attacks.

Daly's research helps save lives as people learn how to eat more healthful foods to reduce the risk of getting cancer or having heart attacks. She also helped create programs to get more people of color into medical school and other science programs.

A scientist working in a laboratory

FIGHTING CANCER

Taiwanese American scientist Jacqueline Whang-Peng is known work in oncology—the research and treatment of cancer. She as a researcher at the National Cancer Institute for over thirty and won many science awards.

the NIH Record

U. S. DEPARTMENT OF HEALTH, EDUCATION, AND WELFARE

March 1, 1972
Vol. XXIV, No. 5

NATIONAL INSTITUTES OF HEALTH

Dr. P.L. Eichman Named BHME Deputy Director

Dr. Peter L. Eichman, coordinator of Health Affairs of the University of Wisconsin Medical School, has been named deputy director of the Bureau of Health Manpower Education. Dr. Eichman was formerly dean of the school.

For the past 4 years, Dr. Eichman has been a member of a BHME committee that reviews grants to schools of medicine and osteopathy.

He has been director of the University of Wisconsin Medical Center and professor of Medicine and Neurology. He has also been a member of the Wisconsin Governor's Committee on Employ-

Dr. Eichman has published a number of articles in the fields of neurology and internal medicine.

ment of the Handicapped.

Dr. Eichman, who received his M. D. degree from Jefferson Medical College, joined the University of Wisconsin Medical School faculty 17 years ago after completing his residency in neurology and internal medicine at the Mayo Clinic.

He has been certified by the American Board of Psychiatry and Neurology and the American Board of Internal Medicine.

The new deputy director was active in regional and state planning committees dealing with health manpower and health care problems.

Carl A. Fretts to Direct Expanded NCI Program Of Research Contracts

Carl A. Fretts has been appointed chief of the Research Contracts Branch, National Cancer Institute. He will be responsible for the business management of NCI's expanded contract program.

Mr. Fretts previously served at NCI from 1965 to 1970 as special assistant for business administration to Dr. C. Gordon Zubrod, NCI's scientific director for Chemotherapy. In June 1970 he received the DHEW Superior Service Award.

Was DuVal Aide

Mr. Fretts has since served as executive officer to Dr. Merlin K. DuVal, HEW Assistant Secretary for Health and Scientific Affairs. He was also executive officer to Dr. Roger O. Egeberg when Dr. Egeberg occupied that office.

He most recently headed the National Science Foundation's Management and Cost Analysis Staff in NSF's Grants and Contracts office.

Mr. Fretts, a certified Certified public

(See MR. FRETTS, Page 4)

Drs. Asofsky and Whang-Peng Presented With Flemming Award for Their Studies

Two NIH researchers—Drs. Richard M. Asofsky and Jacqueline Whang-Peng—were presented with the Arthur S. Flemming Award, honoring outstanding young men and women in the Federal Government. Earlier, both had been nominated for the prestigious award.

Dr. Asofsky is with the National Institute of Allergy and Infectious Diseases. Dr. Whang-Peng, National Cancer Institute, was one of two women to re-

ceive the award. This year, for the first time, women were eligible to enter as nominees.

The 10 Flemming Award winners—five in scientific fields—were presented with engraved plaques by Dr. Arthur S. Flemming, Special Consultant to the President on Aging. The ceremony took place at a luncheon in the Mayflower Hotel, Washington, D. C., on Feb. 11.

HEW Under Secretary John G. Veneman, representing Secretary Elliot L. Richardson, gave the principal address. He commended the awardees for their work, which he described as having "far-reaching impact."

Among the NIH representa-

(Continued on Page 2)

Dr. Alvin Weinberg Gives NIH Lecture on March 15

Dr. Alvin M. Weinberg, Director of the Oak Ridge National Laboratory, will present the next NIH Lecture on Wednesday, March 15, at 8:15 p.m., in the Jack Masur Auditorium, Clinical Center.

Dr. Weinberg will speak on "Science and Trans-Science."

NIH to Implement U.S.-U.S.S.R. Agreement To Collaborate on Research in 3 Areas

Anatoly F. Dobrynin, Soviet Ambassador to the U.S., announces the agreement between the United States and the Soviet Union to collaborate in research on cancer, heart disease, and environmental problems. Seated l to r are HEW Secy. Richardson; Jacob Beam, U.S. Ambassador to Russia; Dr. Egeberg; Dr. Marston, and Dr. Ehrlich.

The National Institutes of Health will assist in the implementation of a new agreement between the United States and the Soviet Union to expand collaboration in the study of cancer, heart disease, and environmental problems, HEW Secretary Elliot L. Richardson announced at a press conference held Feb. 11.

The NIH components designated by the Secretary for carrying out programs in these three areas are the National Heart and Lung Institute, the National Cancer Institute, the National Institute of Environmental Health Sciences, and the Fogarty International Center.

Plan Early Meeting

The collaboration will be initiated through a U.S.-U.S.S.R. Joint Committee for Health Cooperation which is expected to meet for the first time in Moscow in mid-March.

Dr. Roger O. Egeberg, Consultant to the President and Special Assistant to the Secretary, has been designated American Co-Chairman of the Joint Committee.

Dr. Paul S. Ehrlich, Director of the Office of International Health, is American assistant co-chairman.

Included in the delegation to

(See RESEARCH AGREEMENT, Page 6)

An article talking about Jacqueline Whang-Peng winning the Flemming Award in 1972 for her work

CHAPTER 2

Making Change in Technology

From artificial intelligence (AI) to computer systems, women advance technology to help address everyday challenges.

New Ideas

In 2005 Hurricane Katrina hit the southeastern US. It damaged roads, homes, and businesses. Engineer Marian Rogers Croak made a new technology in response to the natural disaster. It was a texting program that allowed people to text donations to help people after natural disasters.

Croak has over two hundred patents. One of them is for Voice over Internet Protocol (VoIP). This technology makes it possible for people to make phone calls through the internet and on apps such as Zoom and FaceTime. In 2022 Croak became one of the first two Black women to join the National Inventors Hall of Fame. She serves as a vice president at Google.

Google vice presidents Marian Croak and James Manyika (*left*) speak at an event in 2022.

HOME SECURITY SYSTEMS

Marie Van Brittan Brown and her husband, Albert Brown, invented a home security model in 1966. It had video cameras, microphones, an emergency button to alert the police, and a remote to unlock doors. She received an award for her work. This model has been used in thirty-two other patented designs for modern-day home security systems.

Making the Internet Possible

Radia Perlman is an engineer and expert in math. Many people call Perlman the mother of the internet because her work helped make the internet possible. She helped create the systems needed for computers to share information with one another. She has spent her career making and improving computer networks.

Perlman holds over one hundred patents and has won many computer science awards. She joined the National Inventors Hall of Fame in 2016.

Engineer Radia Perlman

EARLY COMPUTER PROGRAMMER

Josephine Jue (*below*) was one of the first Asian American compute
programmers. She worked on space shuttle systems at the Nationa
Aeronautics and Space Administration (NASA) for over thirty years

> **"We have a voice and a choice in the kind of future we have."**
>
> —JOY BUOLAMWINI, 2020

Poet of Code

Computer scientist Joy Buolamwini calls herself a poet of code. She combines the arts with science to fight for justice. Her research addresses gender and race bias in AI. This technology mirrors human thinking to do tasks.

Buolamwini did a study to show that AI could only recognize the faces of people from certain races. That means faces will not always be identified correctly. So she founded the Algorithmic Justice League. The group looks at the harms of AI and educates people about the problem.

Joy Buolamwini speaks at the 2019 Bloomberg Equality Summit.

CHAPTER 3

Solving Problems in Engineering

Engineers design and build machines. They are leaders in problem-solving.

New Products

After graduating from college, Uma Chowdhry moved from India to the US and her passion for science grew. She spent most of her career working at DuPont, a chemicals company. She worked on many research projects. For one project, she used ceramics as a conductor—an object that allows the flow of electricity.

Chowdhry joined the National Academy of Engineering in 1996 and the American Academy of Arts and Sciences in 2003.

Uma Chowdhry attends the 2008 World Economic Forum.

A LOCKHEED PROJECT

Mary Golda Ross, a member of the Cherokee Nation, was the first known Native American female engineer. She was one of the first members of the Skunk Works project at Lockheed, an aerospace company. There she explored ideas for space travel and how to reac[h] Mars and Venus. She spent her later years working to get more youn[g] women and Native Americans interested in STEM.

Aircraft such as this one were created as a part of Skunk Works.

"Math was more fun than anything else. It was always a game for me."

—MARY GOLDA ROSS

Breast Cancer Research

Nola Hylton is an oncologist and a leader in breast cancer research. Over the past two decades, she has done research to improve the technology that detects breast cancer. She also looks at the disease's response to treatment.

Hylton has written many articles about her work and has received many awards. She is a professor in the school of medicine at the University of California, San Francisco.

Nola Hylton works to improve technology that detects breast cancer.

Cynthia Breazeal with the social robot Jibo in 2015

Future Robotics

Cynthia Breazeal is a robotics engineer. She focuses on human interactions with robots and social robots. A social robot has an AI system designed to interact with humans and other robots. Breazeal made the social robot Kismet in the late 1990s. Kismet was made to recognize and express human emotions.

FUTURE LEADER

Energy engineer Zoë Penko won the Society of Women Engineers' Rising Star Award in 2019. The award is given to college engineers who have made great achievements in the field.

Students working on an engineering project

Breazeal is a professor and runs the Personal Robots group at the Massachusetts Institute of Technology. She also works to make AI education available to everyone. She has received many awards for her robots and robotics research.

CHAPTER 4

Leading Change in Math

Women use math in many fields, including medicine and computer programming. They use math to research and answer questions.

Making Directions

Gladys West was an expert in math. She programmed computers to solve problems using math. In 1979 she became the manager of the Seasat project. Seasat was a satellite that could monitor Earth's oceans.

West also programmed a computer to use math and make a model of Earth. This led to the technology behind the Global Positioning System (GPS). People use GPS for directions and to find where things are anywhere in the world. In 2018 West was honored for her work by being inducted into the United States Air Force Space and Missiles Pioneers Hall of Fame.

Gladys West receives an award during a ceremony to honor her joining the US Air Force Space and Missiles Pioneers Hall of Fame.

INCREASING DIVERSITY

Math expert Alison Brown (*below*) is the president of the Science Museum of Minnesota. She works to increase the number of women and people of color in STEM through programs and reaching out to the community.

Maryam Mirzakhani (*center*) receives the Fields Medal in 2014.

Math Firsts

Maryam Mirzakhani was an Iranian math expert with a career of firsts. She was the first Iranian woman to compete on a math Olympiad team. In 1994 and 1995, she won gold medals

> "The most rewarding part is the 'Aha' moment, the excitement of discovery and enjoyment of understanding something new— the feeling of being on top of a hill and having a clear view."
>
> —MARYAM MIRZAKHANI, 2014

at the International Mathematical Olympiad, a world math competition for high school students held each year.

Mirzakhani got her PhD from Harvard University in 2004. Ten years later, she became the first woman and the first Iranian to be awarded the Fields Medal. The Fields Medal is given for achievements in math. She worked as a professor at Princeton University and Stanford University before she died in 2017 from breast cancer.

CONCLUSION

STEM Changes Lives

Emmanuelle Charpentier and Jennifer A. Doudna's research led to the discovery of genetic scissors. This tool will aid in separating and cutting DNA to prevent the spread of diseases such as cancer. This is just one example of how STEM can change lives. Women all around the world are leading change in STEM every day. You can be a leader in STEM too!

Emmanuelle Charpentier (*left*) and Jennifer A. Doudna (*right*) win the 2017 Japan Prize.

Glossary

artificial intelligence (AI): technology that mirrors human behavior

computer programmer: someone who writes instructions for a computer to follow

computer science: the study of computers and computer systems

engineer: someone who creates, designs, or builds technologies

interact: to respond to others in a social situation

justice: to be fair or right

oncology: the research and treatment of cancer

patent: a license granted by the government that gives someone the right to make, use, or sell an invention

robotics: the technology of designing, building, and using robots

scientist: an expert who explores natural or physical sciences

technology: machinery and products that use science to solve problems

Source Notes

16 Amy Farley, "Meet the Computer Scientist and Activist Who Got Big Tech to Stand Down," *Fast Company*, August 4, 2020, https://www .fastcompany.com/90525023/most-creative-people-2020-joy -buolamwini.

19 Shane Croucher, "Who Was Mary G. Ross? Facts and Quotes about the First Female Native American Engineer Celebrated in a Google Doodle," *Newsweek*, August 9, 2018, https://www.newsweek.com /mary-g-ross-google-doodle-1064895.

27   "Maryam Mirzakhani: 'The More I Spent Time on Maths, the More
     Excited I Got,'" *Guardian* (US edition), August 12, 2014, https://www
     .theguardian.com/science/2014/aug/13/interview-maryam
     -mirzakhani-fields-medal-winner-mathematician.

Learn More

Biography: Marie M. Daly
https://www.biography.com/scientists/marie-m-daly

Britannica Kids: Mary Golda Ross
https://kids.britannica.com/kids/article/Mary-Golda-Ross/633434

Freeman, Martha. *Born Curious: 20 Girls Who Grew Up to be Awesome
Scientists*. New York: Simon & Schuster Books for Young Readers, 2020.

National Geographic: Women in STEM
https://education.nationalgeographic.org/resource/women-stem/

National Park Service: Women in Science Stories
https://www.nps.gov/nature/daretoimagine.htm

Shepherd, Crown. *Changemakers in Space: Women Leading the Way*.
Minneapolis: Lerner Publications, 2024.

Sneideman, Joshua, and Erin Twamley. *Everyday Superheroes: Women in
STEM Careers*. Minneapolis: Wise Ink, 2019.

Tyner, Dr. Artika R. *Black Achievements in STEM: Celebrating Katherine
Johnson, Robert D. Bullard, and More*. Minneapolis: Lerner Publications,
2024.

Index

Photo Acknowledgments

Images used: J. Lawler Duggan/For The Washington Post/Getty Images, p.5; AIP
Emilio Segrè Visual Archives, Gift of Bill Woodward, USNS Kane Collection, p.7;
Iseo Yang/Getty Images, p.8; IanDagnall Computing/Alamy, p.9; sanjeri/Getty
Images, p.10; National Institutes of Health/Department of Health and Human
Services, p.11; AP Photo/John Minchillo, p.13; Courtesy of Radia Perlman, p.14;
NASA/JSC, p.15; Bess Adler/Bloomberg/Getty Images, p.16; Adrian Moser/
Bloomberg/Getty Images, p.18; U.S. Airforce, p. 19; Courtesy of Nola Hylton,
p.20; Matthew Cavanaugh for The Washington Post/Getty Images, p.21; Monkey
Business Images/Shutterstock, p.22; US Air Force photo by Adrian Cadiz, p.24;
© Glen Stubbe/Minneapolis Star Tribune via ZUMA Wire/Alamy, p.25; AP Photo/
Lee Young Ho/Pool/Sipa USA, p.26; Kyodo News Stills/Getty Images, p.29. Design
elements: Old Man Stocker/Shutterstock; MPFphotography/Shutterstock; schab/
Shutterstock.

Cover: Tibrina Hobson/Getty Images; Lane Turner/The Boston Globe/Getty
Images.